All things bright and beautiful

All creatures great and small

All things wise and wonderful

The Lord God made them all.

— Cecil Francis Alexander, 1848

Butterfly Wings

Thoughts that will let you Soar!

Betty
Parsonage

Blessings
Betty Parsonage

Published by:

Printcorp. LP # 347 of 11.05.99. Minsk. Belarus. Ord. 02158. Qty 5 000 cps.

Acknowledgments

A heartfelt thank you...

to my family and friends for their support and encouragement . . .

to my art teachers whose patience and guidance helped me create the paintings in this book . . .

and to God my creator for the inspiration and the words.

10% of the profits from the sale of this book will go to the North American Butterfly Association.

Contents

Introduction

The butterfly has been a symbol of spiritual growth from the Egyptians to modern man. There is something extremely intriguing about "metamorphosis," the butterfly's life cycle, and its correlation to man's own personal growth.

I have "raised" butterflies for a number of years. Still, the process of metamorphosis is just as exciting today as it was the first time I had the privilege of invading mother nature's privacy to witness this phenomenal event. It is always early morning when a butterfly breaks out of its chrysalis and spreads its wings for the first time. Each time I witness this miraculous birth, I am in awe and reminded that with each new day, I, too, am given the opportunity of a new beginning.

When it was suggested to me that I write and illustrate a book about butterflies, the concept seemed totally out of my range of comprehension. However, the idea stayed with me and I started sorting through the endless stacks of information I had accumulated over the years. Soon my goal became the creation of a book, written in an interesting enough fashion, that one would not have to be a budding naturalist to be inspired.

As I started putting notes down on paper, I also realized, as with my painting and poetry, that I wasn't really writing anything myself. I was simply the conduit for thoughts and ideas coming from a source far greater than my own.

As I wrote, it became clear to me once again that butterflies are truly the most magnificent creatures. Not like any other living thing known to man, except perhaps man himself. Mary Antin wrote in 1912: "We are not born all at once, but by bits. The body first, and the spirit later." Think about how different we are as adults than when we were children. We, too, start out as an egg, are born, crawl like a caterpillar and then many times throughout our lives shed our skin so a new one will grow. Finally, we emerge as something far greater and more beautiful than we could have ever imagined.

I hope you, too, will marvel at the wonder of the butterfly's existence. But remember that our own existence is so much more magnificent, and if we will just ask for the guidance and direction that is ours and ours alone... We, too, will soar! You will find as you "learn" more about butterflies, you will "see" more butterflies. This is just one of the phenomenon's of life. I hope you enjoy reading this book as much as I have enjoyed creating it.

Betty Parsonage

Lepidoptera . . .

The scientific name or order that has been given to butterflies and moths.

Butterflies are flying insects, the most diverse organisms on earth. They account for nine-tenths of all living things, and without them life as we know it would not exist.

All insects have an "external" skeleton, three main body parts and six legs. However, butterflies are unique because they have scales that cover their wings and body. Butterflies are surely the most recognizable and beautiful of all insects. The name "butterfly" probably came from the buttery yellow color of a very common European butterfly that is similar to our yellow Sulphur. It is interesting to note, since the average butterfly lives only a few weeks, that butterflies have survived for almost 40 million years. Butterfly prints found in fossil beds in Colorado and paintings of butterflies in Egyptian tombs confirm this.

There are 20,000 species of butterflies in the world today, 750 in the U.S. and Canada, no two exactly alike. Thousands more are yet to be identified and named. Each one is a perfect example of God's exquisite creativity.

Stay near me - do not take thy flight,

A little longer stay in sight.

Much converse do I find in thee

Historian of my infancy.

— William Wordsworth

The Magic of Metamorphosis . . .
From Egg to Caterpillar

The butterfly's life cycle begins when a female butterfly lays a tiny egg or eggs on the underside of a leaf. The amazing thing is that the butterfly will only lay her eggs on the one specific plant that will provide the correct food source for her caterpillars when they emerge.

The emerging caterpillar (larva) is a unique creature in its own right. It has a voracious appetite and doesn't do much more than eat and sleep during this phase. Caterpillars are equipped with huge jaws for chewing and sometimes are so loud you can actually hear them eating if you listen carefully. The caterpillar's skin cannot stretch as it grows. So it sheds its skin, or molts, five or six times during its short life - an average of two to four weeks. Prior to shedding its skin for the last time, the caterpillar weaves a thread of fine silk. It then attaches itself to a twig or leaf before transforming into a chrysalis — its final stage before becoming a butterfly.

What a caterpillar calls the end of the world,

The Master calls a butterfly.

— Richard Bach

From Chrysalis (Pupae) to Butterfly

This is the most vulnerable stage in the butterfly's life cycle and a time of total transformation. The once wormlike caterpillar liquefies and then rebuilds itself, cell by cell, into a beautiful butterfly. As the butterfly develops, you can see the shape of its wings and body take form through the semi-transparent chrysalis.

When the butterfly is fully developed, the chrysalis splits open and the adult butterfly emerges. The first half-hour or so of its new life is critical to its survival. The butterfly must hang upside down and quickly pump fluid into its wings before they harden. (If this does not happen, the butterfly will never fly.) Soon the "infant adult" will take its maiden flight in search of sweet-smelling nectar and a mate to start its life cycle once again.

True life is lived when tiny changes occur.

— Leo Tolstoy

Metamorphosis

You come from an egg too tiny to see
That was laid on a leaf at the tip of a tree.

You stay t hat way for a number of days.
When the time is right, you end that phase.

A caterpillar next — not the beauty you'll be.
You've more growing to do, before the world is to see.

You spend your days just crawling around,
Eating leaf after leaf high above ground.

Many times as the days come and go,
You shed your skin so a new one will grow.

You think life is great but sense there's much more
You know you must risk, if you're going to soar.

So a home of fine silk you begin to weave
To keep yourself safe, as the past you must leave.

One final time, you change who you are
And emerge from a sleep much different by far.

You flutter your wings and fly to the sky
This freedom you've earned — wasn't something to buy.

For if you had been unwilling to risk,
Just think of the future you would have missed.

So the lesson here for each one to know
Is to shed a few layers and be willing to grow.

— B. Parsonage

One of Life's Lessons

You may have heard this story before, but the lesson is worth repeating. A man was out walking in the woods when he came upon a butterfly struggling to work its way out of its partially opened chrysalis. In what he thought was a kind gesture, the man cut open the chrysalis and gave the little butterfly its freedom. Unfortunately, the man did not understand that the butterfly's struggle was a necessary part of its development and ultimate ability to fly. Without this struggle, the butterfly's wings did not develop, and therefore it was never able to experience the thrill of flight.

How often have we struggled with our own difficult situations, not knowing the reason why? But like the butterfly, our challenges are part of our own transformation and personal growth; without them, we could never develop our wings and learn to fly.

Within every challenge is a gift – let God reveal it.

— Author unknown

Butterfly Families — Who's Who

I have always found it very confusing to decipher, let alone remember, the scientific categorization of butterflies. The names are Latin (many actually derived from Greek mythology) and are comprised of two parts. The first part being the genus, or family, and the second part, the species. The species may then be further divided into hundreds of subspecies. Fortunately, in addition to the scientific names, butterflies have also been given fanciful, common names, like "Painted Lady, Anglewings and Pearl Crescent."

To simplify things, I've used the more recognizable "common names" to introduce you to some of the interesting facts that distinguish one butterfly family from another. (This is by no means a complete list). So... the next time a beautiful little butterfly demands your attention by waving its wings in your direction, you can flatter it by knowing its name.

Swallowtails are some of the largest, most colorful and graceful butterflies on earth. Regardless of where you live, you will have at least one or two types of Swallowtails residing in your area. Swallowtails are easily recognized, by what else but their "tails," which are actually projections from their lower wings. This protruding tail is often relinquished to a predator in lieu of its head or more important body part.

Considering butterflies are delicate little creatures, some Swallowtails have been given rather ferocious names. One of the most beautiful Swallowtails, the "Tiger," is identified by its solid yellow wings. "Zebra" Swallowtails feature black and white zebra-like stripes. The "Giant" Swallowtails have yellow markings on their borders and diagonally across their wings, with an orange dot on the center of each tail. There are many other Swallowtails with more gentle names — the Pipevine, Spicebush and Palamedes, to name a few.

An interesting survival strategy used by the Pipevine Swallowtails (and many other butterfly species as well) is that the butterfly's caterpillar feeds on a plant that contains a very distasteful chemical. This chemical is passed from the caterpillar to the adult butterfly which makes the adult butterfly distasteful to its predators. Many other butterflies then evolve to mimic, or look like, the bad-tasting butterfly. This, of course, helps increase their chances of survival.

Sulphurs and *Whites* like bright, sunny locations and are some of the more common butterflies flitting about your garden. These tiny flying jewels appear in early spring and survive year-round in the South. There are hundreds of different Sulphur species; most are usually solid yellow, orange or white. Solid-color butterflies are somewhat unique since most butterflies have intricate patterns and designs on their wings. Sulphur caterpillars feed on vegetables such as legumes, alfalfa, cabbage and wild mustard and can be a nuisance to farmers. Our little yellow Sulphur is cousin to the "butter yellow" Brimstone found in the English countryside. The Brimstone takes credit for the name "butterfly."

Sulphurs are prone to seasonal variations in color, which is another evolutionary adaptation. In the spring and fall, the Sulphurs need to soak up more of the sun's warmth so they are darker in color than in mid-summer when it is warmer and they are lighter in color.

The family of *Gossamer-Winged* butterflies includes Hairstreaks, Blues, Coppers and Metalmarks; all are small and frail in appearance. Hairstreaks are tiny butterflies with delicate wings that are often hard to spot. Their small size and dull, drab brown or grey color blends well with their environment. There are some, however, usually found only in the tropics, that are showcased with reflective, metallic colors. The green Olive Hairstreak and Great Purple Hairstreak, with their rich royal blue or purple wings, are both quite colorful.

Like Swallowtails, many Hairstreaks have evolved to survive attacks from their predators in an interesting fashion. Instead of tasting bad like the Swallowtails, they have developed what scientists have dubbed "front-to-back mimicry." The Hairstreak's tail looks like its head - their back wings have extensions that look like antenna and spots that resemble eyes. As the butterfly feeds with its head down, its tail is what a predator sees. A butterfly can live with a bit of its tail missing much easier than a bit of its head!

Blues are small iridescent gems with beautifully descriptive names such as Spring Azure Blue and Silvery Blue. Unfortunately, the Silvery Blue, last seen in 1934 in San Francisco, is a casualty of urban development. The smallest butterfly in the world is the Pygmy Blue with a wingspan of less than half an inch.

Little Coppers, with their light-refracting iridescent scales, and Metalmarks, with their metallic gold and blue markings, are dazzling sights if you can catch a glimpse of them during their fast erratic flights.

Brush-Footed butterflies are a very large family of butterflies with a wide variety of sizes and color. Their name comes from the fact that their small front legs are covered with brush-like scales. These "brushes" are not used for walking but rather to scratch the surface of plant leaves in an effort to find the correct plant for the female to lay her eggs on.

Within this family are Longwings — the Julia, Zebras and Gulf Fritillary. Longwings choose passionflowers as their larva plants. Like the pipevine plant, the passionvine contains a poisonous substance that is passed from the caterpillar to the adult butterfly, thus making it distasteful to birds and other predators.

Zebra Longwings have the unusual ability to gather and ingest pollen, which is a protein. Having a diet that includes protein, rather than just the normal butterfly diet of sugary nectar, allows the Zebra to live a much longer life, sometimes as long as five months. This smart little butterfly is the "official" butterfly for the state of Florida.

Anglewings (the genus name means many angles) is so named because of the shape of its wings. These butterflies feed on sap rather than nectar, so you are not as likely to see them in your garden. When they are not in flight and their wings are closed, it is almost impossible to distinguish them from leaves or tree bark.

The very colorful Buckeye does not like the cold, so it resides in the South most of the year only venturing North in the summer. Buckeyes have what are known as "eyespots" on their fore and hind wings. Eyespots are the Buckeye's protective adaptation, serving to confuse a predator in hopes that it might take a bite of its wing rather than its head.

The Mourning Cloaks are the most common member of the Brush-Footed butterflies and are found everywhere in the United States except southern Florida and California. They are the first butterflies you will see in the spring and may even be seen on a warm winter day. They have the capability to fly when the temperatures are in the low 60's. (Most butterflies prefer a temperature of at least 70° to take flight.) The Mourning Cloaks, with the longest life span of any butterfly, may live as long as ten months. Because of their long life, you will often see them with very tattered wings. A butterfly can actually fly with almost half of either wing gone.

The male Red Admiral probably derived its name from the uniform of an English naval officer — blue or black background with white spots. Or perhaps it was because of the territorial nature of these little butterflies. They "stand guard" over their claimed territory and have been known to chase birds and other butterflies out of their area. They will even "check out" a human invader. The Red Admiral has a reputation of visiting the same spot, at the same time each day, for days in a row.

Henry Swanson, in his book *Butterfly Revelations*, gives an account of over 4,400 Red Admiral visitations to his backyard spanning a period of twenty years. This sheer number of visits is amazing; however, two things make it even more so. One is that Mr. Swanson lives in a very urbanized area in Central Florida with lots of traffic. His backyard is void of any nectar or larva plants and is small and surrounded by very tall trees which provide a lot of shade. There is nothing in his yard to encourage a butterfly visit. And secondly, these butterfly encounters started at the same time Mr. Swanson was planning his retirement years and wondering how he would spend his free time. Mr. Swanson believes "God works in mysterious ways, and this was God's way of strengthening his faith and helping him rearrange his goals in life."

The Red Admiral's caterpillars spend their winters curled up in the base of a leaf that is secured to a twig. If you see a tiny bit of a leaf that is still attached to a twig on an otherwise bare branch, you have probably found an Admiral caterpillar's winter home. At the first sign of spring the caterpillar will wake up and continue life where it left off.

The American Painted Lady, also known as the "Cosmopolite," is another well-known butterfly with a world-wide distribution. The Painted Lady is found on every continent except Antarctica and has one of the greatest ranges and migratory patterns of any butterfly.

The *Milkweed* butterflies are the most popular and best-known family of butterflies. Their names — Monarch, Queen and Soldier — attest to the royal status they have been given in the human's view of the butterfly world. The Monarch has been "nominated" as our national insect. Milkweed butterflies use the same survival strategy as the Swallowtails; their caterpillars eat a very distasteful plant, the milkweed, and pass the bad-tasting poison on to the adult butterfly. The Monarchs, sometimes called the "Wanderers" are very strong fliers and are the master of migration, which has become another topic of great interest and research . . . .

*There are only two ways
to live your life
One is as though nothing
is a miracle;
The other is as though
everything is a miracle.*

— Albert Einstein

The Monarch's Magnificent Migration

The Monarch's migration is a mystery of nature! Twice a year the Monarchs embark on a 2,000-mile trip that will take them "home." It can take up to four generations of Monarchs to reach their final destination — the butterfly that starts the trip is not the butterfly that ends the trip! How can something with a wingspan of four inches travel so far, and how do they know where to go?

We don't know. We can only speculate. This is truly one of God's secrets. Some scientists believe the Monarchs have a built-in compass to point them in the right direction. Or perhaps they navigate by using the sun. Another theory known as "collective memory" or "morphic resonance" postulates that when a certain behavior is repeated often enough within a species, it is in some way transmitted (as if by magic through time and space) to other members of the same species. (If true, think about the ramifications this theory has on the human race. Our behaviors today, both good and bad, will automatically be passed on to the next generation!)

We don't know how the Monarchs know where to go, but we do know that as many as 250 million of them make their way to the California coast or Central Mexico in the fall, and their children or grandchildren return to "make their way home" in the spring.

God's Palette

Butterflies attract our attention because of their beautiful display of colors and patterns. The color of a butterfly's wing comes from either pigment in the scales or because the scales refract light, much the way a prism does. This refracted light sometimes makes the colors seem iridescent.

Even though a butterfly is usually not comprised of more than five colors, the varying intensity of a single color and its overlapping scales (placing one color on top of another) create a palette that would entice any artist. Some butterflies change color from one generation (brood) to the next. Sulphurs, for example, are bright yellow in the summer sun but almost tan as fall arrives.

Male butterflies are usually the most colorful, some contain ultraviolet colors that can only be seen by other butterflies. Females tend to blend more with their surroundings, which helps camouflage them from predators. Many butterflies have bright colors on the upper surface of their wings but what are called "cryptic colors" on the underside. Cryptic colors are colors that resemble and blend with the surroundings, such as tree bark or leaves.

As an artist, I'm most intrigued with a butterfly's colors. It's as if God followed all the "rules" of color theory when He colored their wings. Look at the Red Spotted Purple (which is actually not red or purple). This beautiful butterfly has brilliant blue wings with a splash of orange (orange is the complement of blue and, therefore, the ideal accent color).

Or the little Sulphurs with their expressive monochromatic color scheme consisting of shades of yellow ranging from pale lemon to orange. Our world is truly blessed with infinite beauty by our Creator.

In the beauty of a butterfly one can plainly see,
That God is all around us – believing is the key.

— B. Parsonage

Seasons

Butterflies live anywhere from one week to many months. Their life cycle is synchronized with the seasons and is a determining factor in how long they live.

The air temperature must be at least 60°, preferably warmer, for butterflies to be active, and the butterfly's body temperature must be at least 85°. Sometimes you may see butterflies resting or "basking" with their wings outstretched, perpendicular to the sun's rays, literally "soaking up the sun" in an effort to raise their body temperature.

In the wintertime butterflies hibernate (diapause) in a variety of ways. A few, like the Monarch, fly to Mexico or Southern California, some spend the winter as caterpillars, others in the chrysalis stage. A few hibernate as adult butterflies so they are ready to appear at the first sign of spring.

There is a time
for everything,
and a season
for every activity
under heaven.
—Ecclesiastes 3:1

New International Version

The Master of Creativity

Kjell Sandved, a naturalist, sociologist and a staff photographer for the Smithsonian Institute, has chased and photographed the elusive butterfly for over thirty years. He found so much diversity on the wings of butterflies and moths that he actually identified all twenty-six letters of the alphabet and the numbers one through nine.

His venture began when he found a perfectly formed "F" on the wing of a moth and ended when he found the letter "R" on the wing of a butterfly that had been keeping a "low profile" in Africa.

Sandved believes "The butterfly is the symbol of the soul, it is vulnerable, beautiful and delicate." He says that "Butterfly wings are like our fingerprints, there are no two exactly alike."

Tallahassee Democrat, Features, July 15, 1991

Just as each butterfly is a magnificent, "one of a kind," original, so are we!

Each one of us is God's special work of art

— Joni Eareckson Tada

A Butterfly's Inspiration

Here is a beautiful thought and maybe why so many of us are inspired by butterflies. Butterflies have many natural enemies (birds, other insects, bad weather, man, etc.), but they are not a predator to anyone or anything. Their short time on earth is spent helping the environment by sipping nectar and pollinating flowers, fruits and vegetables. Some flowers are totally dependent on butterflies for pollination.

Maybe we could be more like butterflies? Imagine what our world would be like if we could focus our energies on positive things and release all negative thoughts toward one another - there would be no fighting, no wars, no destruction; our world would surely be a more beautiful place.

Think about this: every time you see a butterfly, imagine it is a tiny messenger from God and give it a loving thought to deliver to someone you love.

... In the shadow
of your wings I will take refuge...

— Psalm 57:1
New American Standard

The Business of Butterflies

You may find this hard to believe, but selling butterflies, (or in this case, caterpillars) really is a business. Lorenzo Zayas, alias "The Butterfly Man," is a degreed entomologist who sells caterpillars for a living — an average of 300 a month. In addition to caterpillars, his inventory includes caterpillar accommodations and a variety of other necessary items to provide the perfect environment for his furry pets. The caterpillars come complete with food and instructions for raising.

"The Butterfly Man" also carries a line of chrysalis. (The chrysalis is the stage of metamorphosis between caterpillar and butterfly.) If you are the impatient type and anxious to witness the birth of your tiny flying pet, purchasing a chrysalis will shorten your wait from weeks to just days.

On any given Saturday you can find "the Butterfly Man" in his booth at a Central Florida farmer's market where there is always a line of enthusiastic people, sometimes eight — ten deep, young and old alike! They are either waiting to make a purchase, ask a butterfly-related question, or just relay a personal butterfly encounter.

By the ever-present smile on "the Butterfly Man's" face, being an entomologist and selling caterpillars must be a great business. I imagine it is because it brings so much happiness to others.

Work is love made visible.

— Kahil Gibran

Happiness is like a butterfly ó
the more you chase it,
the more it will elude you.
But, if you turn your attention
to other things,
the butterfly will come
and sit upon your shoulder.

— Nathaniel Hawthorne

The Endangered Butterfly

In the last fifty years, thousands of species of butterflies have become extinct, many more are endangered and others are less plentiful than they were in the past. Sadly, we are to blame! Every minute of every day, we destroy the equivalent of 50 football fields of tropical rain forest (home to 10,000 species of butterflies). We cut down our forests for timber, and we spray our flowers and vegetables with insecticides that kill the butterflies and caterpillars.

The little El Segunda Blue that once flitted among the sand dunes along the California coast has lost its natural habitat and is now the rarest of all butterflies. It resides in a small 300-acre patch of land beside a runway at the Los Angeles International Airport.

It is up to us to make some changes. One of the most rewarding things we can do is to establish a butterfly garden in our own backyard. It doesn't matter whether we have large yards that can be transformed into havens of sweet-smelling, colorful nectar plants or just a small patio . . . We can make a difference! The reward when that first beautiful butterfly appears is well worth the effort.

The *Butterfly World Official Guide* presents a rather frightening thought: "Butterflies are a most sensitive indicator of the health of our environment. If they can no longer survive in the place we call home, how much longer can we?"

Show love to all creatures
and you will be happy
for when you love all things,
you love the Lord,
for He is all in all.

— Tulsidas

Our Pledge

Your natural beauty is a gift to behold . . .
you never cease to inspire the young or the old.

We watch you in wonder as you flutter around
searching for nectar until it is found.

But the risk that we face, year after year,
is that spring will arrive and you won't be here.

The thing that's ironic, since you bring us such joy,
is we all still continue to disrupt and destroy.

If we'd just replace each time we cut down,
the balance would come and your home would be sound.

So let's make a pledge, before it's too late
to alter our ways and protect your fate.

— B. Parsonage

Butterfly Gardens

Designing a butterfly garden doesn't have to be costly or complicated, but there are some fairly specific rules you will have to follow. The goal is to conserve or re-create, a natural environment where butterflies can survive and prosper.

Butterflies have very discriminating taste. At a minimum, you will need a sunny location, a variety of nutrient-rich nectar plants (food for the adult butterfly) and some tall shrubs, vines or trees to provide a windbreak. If you want the butterflies to stay from one generation to the next, your garden will also have to include "host specific" larva plants for the female butterflies to lay their eggs on. There are a few plants, the Monarch's Milkweed, for example, that is both a nectar and larva plant. Where available, native plants are your best choice.

Most nectar plants have a strong sweet fragrance. However, not all nectar flowers are an acceptable food source to all butterflies. The length of the butterfly's tongue (proboscis) determines which type of flower it can sip nectar from. Butterflies prefer flowers that are red, yellow, blue, white and lavender. Some flowers have the added advantage of possessing distinct ultraviolet patterns that butterflies are able to see. These ultraviolet "road maps" help direct the butterfly to the nectar-laden center of the flower.

Composites, such as daises, are a good choice. They give the butterfly a place to light while sipping nectar from the flower's center. Once you determine the best plants for the butterflies in your area, plant them in mass, rather than scattered throughout your garden. This will make them easier for the butterflies to spot. Consider also the plant's blooming season so when your butterflies show up, breakfast will be waiting.

Each area of the country is different. But one sure way to find out what plants your butterflies like is simply to pay attention to where a butterfly is going when you see one. If you don't know the name of the plant that the butterfly chooses, pick a leaf or flower and take it to your favorite nursery or look it up in a garden book or plant catalogue. (There are many books available on butterfly gardening; however, observing what is already happening in your neighborhood should be your first point of reference.)

Butterfly World in Florida has started a "Bring Back the Butterflies" campaign. For a list of butterfly plants common to your area, just mail a self-addressed stamped envelope to Butterfly World, Tradewinds Park, 3600 West Sample Road, Coconut Creek, Florida 33072, or log onto their Web site at <u>ButterflyWorld.com</u>.

If you want to establish a butterfly garden in your backyard, you must be willing to give up the use of insecticides, and if you have larva plants, you may have to give up the leaves on some plants as well. A few hungry caterpillars can devour a plant quite quickly.

With the rapid growth of urban development, even a small butterfly garden will make a contribution to our environment. We want our children and our children's children to know the beautiful butterfly.

Children need just two things . . .
Roots and Wings

— Author unknown

The Spirit of the Butterfly

Native Americans give special meaning to all of God's creatures and have a natural ability to understand their ways and reasons for being a part of our world and we theirs. They believe butterflies have many lessons to share and we have much to learn about ourselves from watching them, if we will just open our hearts and minds to their teachings.

Great spiritual significance has been given to the miracle of metamorphosis. Symbolically the Native Americans equate metamorphosis to the changes we go through in our lives. They feel we should welcome change, for it is a natural flow of energy and the force behind all creation. They also believe the more we choose to resist change, the more difficult our lives become. We must release the old and embrace the new... When you see a butterfly, look for change.

Native Americans see these delicate creatures as much more than just insects. They feel the butterfly represents the essence of beauty, love and harmony that is everywhere in the world around us.

The earth does not belong to man.
Man belongs to the earth.
All things are connected
like the blood that unites us all.
Man did not weave the web of life;
he is merely a strand in it.
Whatever he does to the web
he does to himself.

— Chief Seattle

If God gave caterpillars wings — imagine his plans for you!!!!

— B. Parsonage

Reprints of the artwork in this
book are available for purchase
at www.striking-designs.com.